Knowing the Real Jesus

Real Questions...
REAL JESUS

Leader's Guide

Χ The Greek Way to Say Jesus

For centuries it has been a symbol for Christ, the anointed one, the Savior. First-century Christians used the Greek letter Χ (pronounced ki or key), which is the first letter in the Greek word for Christ, χριστός (pronounced Kree-stas) as a shorthand for Jesus. The Χ quickly became incorporated into a variety of symbols to represent early Christians' faith in the one God sent, Jesus. It was simple. It pointed to the cross and became a sign identifying believers. The mark and its variation can be found in ancient Roman catacombs, early coins, lamps, and pottery.

Today, Χ still stands for Christ. It is the bridge between the countless number of Christ-followers through history to a new millennium. As young people prepare for the future, they will need the right tools to make sense of a world that often appears senseless. They will need answers to the tough questions. They will need a firm foundation on which to make good decisions about their life and their future. Young people today need the Χ—Jesus.

Through this leader's guide, *Knowing the Real Jesus,* and its companion leader's guides, *Finding the Jesus Experience, Meeting the Jesus Challenge,* and *Discovering the Jesus Answers,* you will be equipped to help young people encounter the *real* Jesus and what he has to say about faith, pain and suffering, relationships, and other issues that touch their lives. In this series of four-week sessions designed for youth group or Sunday school settings, you will be provided with complete lesson outlines on how to communicate to teens who Jesus really is, why he came to earth, and why he deserves their trust, their worship, and their faith.

Χ. One symbol. One hope. One man. One God. One Truth. It's all young people will ever need.

Knowing the Real Jesus

Leader's Guide

David R. Veerman
EMPOWERED® Youth Products

Standard Publishing
Cincinnati, Ohio

All Scripture quotations, unless otherwise indicated, are taken from the *Holy Bible,* New Living Translation, copyright © 1996. Used by permission of Tyndale House Publishers, Inc., Wheaton, IL 60189. All rights reserved.

Developed and produced for Standard Publishing by The Livingstone Corporation. Project staff includes: Kirk Luttrell, Betsy Todt Schmitt, Ashley Taylor, David R. Veerman, and Andrea Reider.

Contributors include: Nate Conrad, Jenny Fichera, Keith Scherer, and Dana Veerman.

Standard Publishing development and editorial team includes: Paul Learned, Darrell Lewis, Dale Reeves, acquisitions editor, and Mark Taylor.

Cover design, Ahaa! Design

Interior design, Mark Wainwright

Copyright © 2002 by Standard Publishing

All rights reserved.

EMPOWERED® Youth Products is a trademark of Standard Publishing.

Printed in the United States of America.

Standard Publishing, Cincinnati, Ohio.

A Division of Standex International Corporation.

09	08	07	06	05	04	03	02
7	6	5	4	3	2	1	

Contents

Introduction   1

session 1
   Knowing Jesus as God   5

session 2
   Knowing Jesus as Man   19

session 3
   Knowing Jesus as Savior   29

session 4
   Knowing Jesus as King   41

The Jesus Experience

The *Real Life ... Real Questions ... Real Jesus* series, consisting of four devotional books and four leader's guides for youth leaders and Sunday school teachers, were written as companion pieces to *The Jesus Bible*. This Bible, published by Tyndale Publishing House and produced and developed by The Livingstone Corporation, was designed to help introduce the Jesus of the Bible to teens in a new and fresh way. *The Jesus Bible* follows the work and purpose of Christ from the Old Testament prophecies about him to his life and ministry on earth. It records Jesus' call to radical living, first voiced about 2,000 years ago, that still resounds today.

Through the features and notes found in *The Jesus Bible,* young people will encounter Jesus in ways they have never experienced before—not the watered-down religious pacifist or the timid-looking person in a stained-glass window. But the Christ, the Messiah, the Savior, the *real* Jesus— in all his color, with all his power, showing up in the most unexpected places and taking the most revolutionary actions. Through *The Jesus Bible,* teens will meet the real Jesus for real life with real answers for life's tough problems.

Why the New Living Translation?

Since its inception, Tyndale House Publishing has been committed to publishing editions of the Bible in the language of the common people. With more than 40 million copies in print, *The Living Bible* represented this tradition for more than 30 years. In recent years, Tyndale continued its commitment and mission by commissioning 90 evangelical scholars to produce the *Holy Bible,* New Living Translation. This general-purpose translation is accurate and excellent for study, yet it is easy to read and understand.

The team of translators was challenged to create a text that would have the same impact in the lives of modern readers as the original text did in the lives of early believers. To accomplish that, the team translated entire thoughts (rather than just words) into natural, everyday English. The result is a translation that speaks to us today in our language, a translation that is easy to understand, and that accurately communicates the meaning of the original texts.

In using the New Living Translation for *The Jesus Bible* and in the *Real Life ... Real Questions ... Real Jesus* series, the publishers at Tyndale House and Standard Publishing pray that this translation will speak to young peoples' hearts and help them understand the Word of God in a fresh and powerful way.

Because you have real questions ... and Jesus has real answers!

INTRODUCTION

A popular television program features three contestants, all claiming to be the same person. When questioned by a panel of celebrities, each one tries to answer in such a way as to get everyone on the panel (and in the television audience) to think that he or she is truly the person described. Eventually, the members of the panel each state who *they* think has answered truthfully. Then the host says, "Will the *real* (person) please stand up!" and the truth is revealed.

Today, many ideas and ideals compete for attention, each claiming to be the truth. Among those competing claims stand Christians proclaiming Jesus. Yet, even when those voices are heard among the noise and confusion, they often present a wide array of views concerning Jesus' identity. Like a twist to the TV quiz show, one view seems to say: "I'm Jesus, the humble, meek, and mild baby in the manger." Another says, "No, *I* am Jesus, the leader and teacher." Still another adds, "You've got it all wrong, *I* am Jesus, the radical martyr!" It's enough to make us scream, "Will the *real* Jesus please stand up!"

"Will the *real* Jesus please stand up!"

Today, no one is more susceptible to this confusion and misconception than young people. As never before, they are assaulted by competing values, lifestyles, religions, and "truths" through countless TV channels, the Internet, and other media, electronic and otherwise. They have a smorgasbord of ideas from which to choose a system of truth, *their* truth.

Yet Jesus stated, "I am the way, the truth, and the life. No one can come to the Father except through me" (John 14:6).

Our challenge as youth leaders is to cut through the verbiage and noise and help our students see Jesus, the *real* Jesus. And that's the purpose of this book—to help you point young people to the Truth.

Each of the four sessions focuses on an important aspect of Jesus' identity.

First, we look at Jesus as God—the fact that Jesus is **fully divine**, not just a human teacher or martyr. If we want to know what God is like, we can look at his Son.

The second session highlights Jesus' **humanity**—the fact that while fully God, Jesus was also fully human. He experienced all that we experience—he knows us thoroughly. And he's a perfect example to follow.

The third session looks at Jesus as **Savior**, underscoring his main purpose for coming to earth. The objective here is to show that Jesus died on the cross to save us from the power and penalty of our sins and to challenge students to trust Christ as the Savior, *their* Savior.

Finally, the last session explores Jesus as **King**, the "King of kings and Lord of lords." Students are encouraged to think of the personal implications of that truth and to acknowledge Jesus as Lord of their lives.

At the beginning of each study, you'll find a number of extras that you can use to lengthen, deepen, or otherwise adapt that lesson to your group. These additions include contemporary music and videos, worship songs, and optional openers.

Since the media (especially music and film) make up a large part of students' identity and often shape their culture, we have included numerous Media Moments. These include music or movie clip suggestions that reinforce the teaching of the day. WARNING! Preview all film clips before using them. They are not always obviously "spiritual" or self-explanatory.

Weave these illustrations into your presentation of the material. Without proper explanation before or after, they might become simply entertainment and not a powerful teaching tool. Also, there could possibly be offensive material before or after the suggested clip, so know when to start and stop it. These choices have been selected with a perspective of "bridging the gap" with unchurched teens and "seekers" with little or no church background. NOTE: The start points noted are from the opening studio logo of the movie, not the beginning of your tape. Reset the counter to 0:00:00 when the studio logo appears.

Groups with access to media will want to plan ahead to secure videos and order CDs. The United States Copyright Act treats displays or performance of multimedia presentations, films, and videotapes by nonprofit organizations (including churches) to a small group of individuals as "public performances" even if no admission fee is charged. The fact that the church or one of its members may have purchased the copy of the film or videotape makes no difference. To avoid running afoul of the "public performance" prohibition in the Copyright Act, you must in each instance secure the copyright owner's permission or alternatively obtain an "umbrella license" from the Motion Picture Licensing Corporation. To learn more about the umbrella license, contact the MPLC at 1-800-462-8855 or visit them on the web at www.mplc.com. You may also want to visit http://fairuse.stanford.edu/ for additional information on the Copyright Act and the "Fair Use Doctrine."

Officially, each session begins with an opening activity under the category of **Real Fun**. As that title implies, the purpose is to have fun together as a group while introducing the theme of the day. Usually that activity will lead to a brief discussion and then, perhaps, to another activity and discussion.

In the next section, **Real Questions**, the group will dive into the topic, using a combination of small groups, worksheets, or another process to facilitate discussion.

Real Jesus, the next section, is the heart of the meeting. Here, through a mixture of talks, Bible study, and discussion, students will discover the person of Christ as he is revealed in Scripture and how he can change their lives.

The focus of the last section, **Real Life**, is application. Here students will be given a way to respond to the lesson, an assignment to help them put the main points into practice.

I have assigned a suggested time for each element of the meeting. If you run the basic lesson with no options and stick to the lowest time, your meeting will be 35 minutes long. Keeping to the higher times for each meeting element will total 50 minutes. Of course, you may want to adjust those and add options to fit the time available.

To help reinforce the weekly sessions and to help students make personal applications, use the devotional book that corresponds to this leader's guide. The book's 30 devotions follow the meetings' themes—one week for "Jesus as God," one week for "Jesus as Man," and so forth.

May God bless you as you lead students in discovering the reality and the implications of knowing the real Jesus.

Dave Veerman

Knowing the Real Jesus

session 1
Knowing Jesus as God

knowing jesus as god — session 1

Notes

> **1A** If you play a CD or a video, be sure to have everything in place and ready to go.

Lesson Texts
Selected passages in the Gospels and 1 Peter 2:22-24

Lesson Focus
Most people have a poor understanding of who Jesus really is, thinking he was just a man who lived 2,000 years ago.

Lesson Goal
As a result of this session, students will know that Jesus was and is fully divine, God in the flesh.

Materials Needed — **1A**
- For *Optional Media Moments*: CD player and TV, VCR, and video
- For *Optional Openers*: quizzes and prizes for *Superhero* and *What Do You Remember?*
- Questions for *What Do You Know?*
- Prize for winning team
- Pictures or symbols of Jesus for *Jesus Is . . .*
- Copies of *Will the Real Jesus Please Stand Up? Worksheet* (one for each person) for *Group Talk*
- Pens and pencils for *Group Talk* and *Response*
- New Testaments for *Group Talk*
- 3" × 5" index cards for *Response*
- Devotional books for *Response*

Media Moments (optional)

Music
- Play "We Are the Champions" by Queen from *Greatest Hits, Vol. 1-2* during **Superheroes**.
- Play "The Glory" by Avalon from their CD, *Oxygen,* or "Surely God Is With Us" by Rich Mullins and a Ragamuffin Band from *The Jesus Record* CD, as students work on their cards in **Response**. Another song that deals with today's topic is "Supernatural," recorded by dc Talk on their *Supernatural* CD.

Video
- Play this clip from *Jesus: The true account of the man who changed history* released by Warner Brothers, A Genesis Project Production, distributed by JVP, 275 Hospitality Lane, Suite 315, San Bernardino, CA 92408. Start the clip approximately six minutes into the video at the sunrise: "Jesus' Public Life." End the clip at the scene fade-out after the Holy Sprit comes down on Jesus and God speaks (about 3 minutes).
- Play this clip from *The Visual Bible—Matthew*: Matthew 8:25—9:8 (tape 1—55:37-59:44 and tape 2—00:08-02:00—6 minutes). In this passage we see Jesus calming the storm, disturbing the pigs, forgiving sins, healing paralysis . . . repeatedly provoking the reaction, "What kind of man is this?"

Worship Songs
- Play one of the following songs before or after the **Response:**
  ① "Come, Now Is the Time to Worship" by Brian Doerksen (on *WOW BLUE WORSHIP* taken from *Winds of Worship 12* from the Vineyard; originally recorded on *Your Love Reaches Me,* #37 in the *Touching the Father's Heart* series from the Vineyard)
  ② "I Believe in Jesus" by Marc Nelson (on *WOW ORANGE WORSHIP* taken from *Change My Heart Oh God, Vol. 1* from the Vineyard)
  ③ "Jesus, Lover of My Soul" by Paul Oakley (on *King of Love: Worship Together Live, Volume 1* from Worship Together and *Passion: The Road to One Day* from Sparrow Records)
  ④ "You Are God" by Scott Underwood (on *WOW ORANGE WORSHIP* taken from *You Are God,* #31 in the *Touching the Father's Heart Series* from the Vineyard)

Notes

1B *The two teams used in all the openers do not have to be exactly the same size, and any combination of students in each team will do. Thus, you can allow sets of friends to remain together if you wish.*

Real Fun
OPTIONAL OPENERS

Superheroes — **1B** (8 min.)

Divide the group into two teams. Have them sit in parallel columns, facing the front. Explain that the first two people in the team columns will compete in the first round of this contest. You will read a clue to the identity of a comic superhero. Whoever (of the two contestants) shouts out the correct superhero first, wins that round. Then those two contestants will go to the back of their respective teams, everyone will move up, and the next two will compete in the next round. Use the following list of clues and their corresponding superheroes in the contest (feel free to add others). Award the winning team 10,000 points (and the "second place team," 5,000 points). Add these points to the totals for the other contests.

Clues	Superheroes
Faster than a speeding bullet	Superman
Web-master	Spider-Man
Angry young man	The Incredible Hulk
Should be water-logged	Aquaman
Female flying rodent	Batgirl
Classic spaceman	Flash Gordon or Buck Rogers
VeggieTales' superhero	Larry-Boy
A cave and a car	Batman
Pimpled reptiles fighting crime	Teenage Mutant Ninja Turtles
Sweet friend for stopping dastardly deeds	Picachu (Pokemon)
Young sidekick	Robin, the Boy Wonder
Muscular Greek guy	Hercules
Amazon woman with an attitude	Xena
360-degree transformation	Wonder Woman

Afterward, take a minute or so to discuss the kinds of heroes we have in society today.

What Do You Remember? (7 min.)

Using two teams, ask trivia questions similar to the ones listed below. (Change this list to make it more or less difficult depending on your group.) Explain that after each question, whoever knows the answer should jump to their feet. Then you will point to the first person to jump and give him or her the chance to answer. You will continue to take answers until you get a correct one or until everyone is stumped. You will award a thousand points to the team of the person with the correct answer.

Use questions like these (the correct answers are in parentheses):
1. What was the Beatles' first big hit in the U.S. in 1964? **("I Want to Hold Your Hand")**
2. Who won the first Super Bowl? **(Green Bay Packers)**
3. Where did the first "Survivor" television show, American version, take place? **(an island in the South Pacific)**
4. What was the original U-2? **(a high-flying reconnaissance plane)**
5. Who was President when you were born?
6. What color were the people the one-eyed, one-horned, flying people-eater ate? **(purple)**
7. Who is the mayor of your town/city?
8. Where were the last two summer Olympics held? **(Atlanta, GA, and Sydney, Australia)**
9. What's the name of Homer Simpson's wife? **(Marge)**
10. Who quarterbacked your high school varsity football team three years ago?
11. Who was vice president under President Clinton? **(Al Gore)**
12. What character did Don Knotts play on "The Andy Griffith Show"? **(Barney Fife)**

Openers

What Do You Know? (5 to 7 min.)

Use the team structure and game procedure as described in the optional opener, **What Do You Remember?** If the person answering a question gives an incorrect answer, however, give his or her team *minus* 500 points; then give the other team the chance to give the correct answer.

Use the following questions and add others to fit your group and the time available (the correct answers are in parentheses).
1. How old was Jesus when his parents found him in the temple talking to the elders? **(12—Luke 2:41-50)**
2. In the wilderness, what did Satan suggest to satisfy Jesus' hunger? **(Jesus should turn stones into bread—Matthew 4:1-4)**
3. What was Jesus' first public miracle? **(He turned water into wine at the wedding in Cana—John 2:1-11)**

Notes

1C For additional student participation, assign students this task of bringing the pictures or symbols and then displaying them when you ask.

1D You may want to print out this passage and give it to a student before the meeting.

4. Which two sets of brothers were among Jesus' first disciples? **(Peter and Andrew, James and John—Matthew 10:1-4)**
5. In the Sermon on the Mount what did Jesus say about cheeks? **(When slapped on one, we should turn to be slapped on the other—Matthew 5:39)**
6. In what village did the "woman at the well" live? **(Sychar—John 4:4-30)**
7. When Jesus and the disciples picked wheat, what did the Pharisees accuse them of doing? **(working on the Sabbath—Luke 6:1-5)**
8. What kinds of stories did Jesus often tell? **(parables—Matthew 13:34-35)**
9. Which two earthly brothers of Jesus each wrote a book of the Bible? **(James and Jude)**
10. What does the name "Christ" mean? **(It is Greek for "Messiah")**

Transition (1 min.)

Determine the winning team and award a prize (or promise a prize for later). Then say something like this: *Can you tell from the last game what our topic is today? That's right—Jesus. I don't know how you did on those questions, but I'll bet you couldn't answer many of them. That's strange, isn't it? Think about it. We say we believe in Christ and that he is our Lord and Savior, but how much do we really know about him? During this session, we're going to look a little closer at his life and learn more about the real Jesus.* Move directly into the next opener.

Jesus Is . . . — 1C (3 to 5 min.)

Bring a number of pictures or symbols of Jesus at various stages of his life on earth. These could include a baby in the manger, talking with the temple leaders, a picture of Jesus from a Bible, a packet of seeds, a picture or story of him throwing out the money-changers from the temple, a carpenter's tool, a crucifix, a stained-glass picture, etc. Display them one at a time and after each one ask: *If this were all you knew about Jesus, what would be your concept of him?* Compile a list of their answers.

Then say something like this: *People today have many different ideas about Jesus, and they get those ideas from many places: artists' ideas, parents, selected Bible stories, friends, TV shows. In Jesus' day, people had different ideas about him too. Listen to this interchange between Jesus and his disciples.*

Talking Points — 1D (6 to 9 min.)

Have someone read aloud Matthew 16:13-15. Thank your reader. Then say: *In the disciples' answer to Jesus' question, they mentioned "John the Baptist" (a* radical preacher), "Elijah" (a famous prophet, long since dead), "Jeremiah" (another dead prophet), or "one of the other prophets." I doubt that people today would give those answers to the question; that is, they wouldn't name those names. But what do you think? What would they say?

Discuss this briefly. Then ask,
- **What concepts do people have about Jesus?** In other words, who do they think he is or was? What do they think he is or was like? **(Possible answers: meek and mild, good example to follow, great moral teacher, counselor, a religious weirdo, 100% God but not man, 100% man but not God, a radical rebel, etc.)**
- **Where do most young people get their ideas about Jesus? (Possible answers: church, parents, movies and TV shows, friends, radio or television preachers, etc.)**
- **In what ways do people use Jesus for their own purposes? (Possible answers: Some invoke his name to support their personal causes, everything from being a vegetarian to being a pacifist. Others discount Jesus and his teachings so they won't feel accountable to him. They might say something like, "Jesus lived so long ago that what he taught doesn't apply to today's issues and technology.")**
- **How can we find out what Jesus is really like? (Answer: check out the Bible.)**

After the discussion, say something like this: *The problem is that everyone wants to put Jesus in a category or slot. If a person can see that Jesus supports his or her cause, then that person feels better about what he or she is doing. Best-selling books describe Jesus as the ideal "businessman," "leader," "revolutionary"—a wide variety of options.*

On the other hand, many people see Jesus as irrelevant; that is, they put him into a specific box so they don't have to consider him. But Jesus doesn't fit into our neat little categories. He won't stay in our intellectual boxes. For many, Jesus is a real threat to their thinking and ways of life.

Ask: *If you want to find out what a person is **really** like, what should you do?* (Answer: talk to people who know that person best and others who have had contact and conversations with him or her, people who have seen the person in action.)

After discussing this briefly, say: *We're going to do exactly that. We are going to go right to the source, to people who walked and talked with Jesus, who heard him, saw him, and touched him. To do this, we will examine the primary historical sources. This will help us discover the real Jesus Christ; it will tell us what he was really like.*

Notes

1E Hopefully, students still will be sitting in their teams; otherwise, it will take time to divide them again.

1F To save time, especially with a large group, give the adult leaders the Bibles, worksheets, and pens and pencils beforehand.

The eyewitness accounts of Jesus' life are included in the books entitled Matthew, Mark, Luke, and John, and in other New Testament books as well.

Real Questions
Group Talk — 1E — 1F   (7 to 10 min.)

Using the two teams from the opener, **What Do You Remember?**, assign each team one half of the **Will the Real Jesus Stand Up? Worksheet** (printed at the end of the lesson) to research. Each team should choose a leader and a secretary. Distribute worksheets to everyone. Explain that students should use their New Testaments to find answers to the questions according to the specific Bible references. After about seven minutes, bring the groups back together to report on their findings. The results should be as follows.

Jesus on Jesus: Jesus made some fantastic claims about himself. These claims are recorded by original eyewitness sources. What were these claims? Jesus claimed . . .

1. to be God (John 10:30-33)
2. to be the only way to the Father (John 14:6)
3. to be the Son of God (Mark 14:61-62)
4. to have power to forgive sins (Mark 2:5-12)
5. to be the same as the Father (John 14:8-9)
6. to fulfill prophecy and to have existed before Abraham (John 8:51-58)

Jesus' contemporaries on Jesus: Other people made statements about Jesus that help us understand him. What did they say?

1. Jewish leaders accused him of making himself equal to God (John 5:16-18).
2. Martha said, "I have always believed you are the Messiah, the Son of God, the one who has come into the world from God" (John 11:25-27).
3. Thomas confessed, "My Lord and my God!" (John 20:28).
4. Peter stated, "You are the Messiah, the Son of the living God" (Matthew 16:16).
5. Peter wrote, "He never sinned, and he never deceived anyone. He did not retaliate when he was insulted. When he suffered, he did not threaten to get even. He left his case in the hands of God, who always judges fairly. He personally carried away our sins in his own body on the cross so we can be dead to sin and live for what is right. You have been healed by his wounds!" (1 Peter 2:22-24).

Real Jesus

Talk-to (3 or 4 min.)

Say something like this: *From our research, we can see that* **Jesus Christ is divine.**

Many people today revere Jesus as a prominent historical figure but merely a man, a human being like you and me. Some highlight Jesus' teachings and promote him as one of the greatest teachers of all time. Others focus on Jesus' moral example and point to him as someone to follow. But in the Gospels record of Jesus' claims and those of his followers, we have just seen that he is much more than that.

He was 100 percent God. He identified himself with his Father; he accepted worship; he claimed certain powers that only God possesses—forgiving sins, casting out demons, raising the dead, knowing the future, etc.; he claimed eternal existence; and more. He wasn't a "super" human or someone acting like God, he was, and is, God—divine, immortal, all-knowing, all-powerful.

Because Jesus is divine, **he is God in focus.** *When the disciples asked Jesus to just show them the Father, Jesus said, "If you had known who I am, then you would have known who my Father is. . . . Anyone who has seen me has seen the Father!" (John 14:7, 9). So when we want to know what God is like, we look at Jesus. God isn't distant and unknowable—he's close, and we can know his character, values, and desires. God is perfectly revealed in Christ.*

Because Jesus is divine, **he is the Savior.** *It is true that Jesus was the greatest moral teacher and example who ever lived and that those who follow his way of life will have peace of mind and live right—but that's only a small part of the story. If Jesus had only been a man, albeit a very good man, his death would have been nothing more than an inspiring example of someone who died for a cause. But because Jesus is divine, his death means something profound—he died for our sin, taking our place on the cross, paying the penalty for our sins. So now everyone who believes in him can be forgiven and become God's child.* — **1G**

And because Jesus is divine, **he now lives to give us a direct way to God.** *Jesus said, "I am going to prepare a place for you. If this were not so, I would tell you plainly. When everything is ready, I will come and get you, so that you will always be with me where I am" (John 14:2-3). And the apostle Paul wrote, "Who then will condemn us? Will Christ Jesus? No, for he is the one who died for us and was raised to life for us and is sitting at the place of*

Notes

> **1G** *Mention that the fact that Jesus is the Savior will be the topic of a future session.*

Notes

> **1H** Remember, it takes time to move in and out of groups.

> **1I** Have extra devotional books available for those who don't have them.

highest honor next to God, pleading for us" (Romans 8:34). *Thus, after we come to Christ by faith and establish this personal relationship with him, through the Holy Spirit we can experience his day-by-day leading in our lives by yielding ourselves to him.*

If Jesus is not who he claimed to be, either he must be a deluded lunatic or the world's greatest imposter. He can't be both a great man and yet merely a man because he claimed to be God. If he claimed to be God but wasn't but didn't know that he wasn't, then Jesus was deluded—mentally challenged. If he claimed to be God but wasn't and knew he wasn't, then Jesus was a liar. The only other option is that he was and is who he claimed to be—God in a human body. The evidence of a perfect life, hundreds of miracles, and his personal resurrection leave only one rational alternative. **He is God!**

Talking Points — **1H** (6 to 9 min.)

Reassemble everyone into the two groups again, and give each group one of the following questions to discuss. Have them record their answers and be ready to present them to the whole group.

- Jesus is God, fully divine—how should this truth affect the way we worship? Pray? Read the Bible?
- Jesus is God, fully divine—how should this truth affect a person's lifestyle? Relationships? Decision-making?

After about three minutes, have the groups report their answers. Then ask: *How should the fact that Jesus is God affect the way we tell others about our faith?* Discuss this briefly.

Real Life

Response — **1I** (4 or 5 min.)

Distribute 3" × 5" index cards and tell everyone to write two or three changes that they will make in their lives now that they are convinced that Jesus is God. (Remind them of the answers to the previous discussion questions.)

Challenge everyone to keep those cards in a place that they will see often, to be a constant reminder (in the Bible, at their desk at school, in the daily schedule, etc.).

Close   (1 min.)

Remind everyone to follow through this week by doing the assigned devotions in book one of the *Real Life . . . Real Questions . . . Real Jesus* series. Explain that this week they will meet Doug with a tough question about his friend Kevin, all-out-and-honest Aaron, Beth in the real world, and others.

Close in prayer.

Junior High Adaptation

Superheroes should work well, but don't use **What Do You Remember?** If you use **What Do You Know?** substitute easier questions (for example, *In what town was Jesus born? What gifts did the Magi bring to baby Jesus? Besides Matthew, Peter, James, and John, what are the names of two more disciples?*) for the more difficult ones. Be sure to move along all the discussions, asking short questions with mostly concrete answers. The discussion groups will work well, but be sure to have an adult for each group. Also, don't distribute worksheets to everyone (they may quickly be destroyed and become a distraction); instead, have the adult leaders assign one or two students in their groups to record the answers. Under **Real Jesus** in the discussion after **Talk-to**, don't go back into the two groups. Instead, keep the whole group together for this discussion.

Will the Real Jesus Please Stand Up?

Section 1

JESUS ON JESUS

Jesus made some fantastic claims concerning who he is. What were come of these claims? Use the following statements from the original sources and summarize the significance of each statement on this sheet.

1. John 10:30-33
2. John 14:6
3. Mark 14:61-62
4. Mark 2:5-12
5. John 14:8-9
6. John 8:51-58

Section 2

JESUS' CONTEMPORARIES ON JESUS

There are several ways to understand or know a person better. We can listen to what that person says about himself or herself. Or we can listen to what others say about him or her. What did other people say about Jesus in the New Testament? Check out these statements and summarize their significance.

1. John 5:16-18
2. John 11:25-27 (also notice what Jesus says about himself)
3. John 20:25-28
4. Matthew 16:15-17
5. 1 Peter 2:22-24

Knowing the Real Jesus

session 2
Knowing Jesus as Man

Lesson Texts
Selected passages in the Gospels; Philippians 2:5-11; Hebrews 4:14-16; 5:8

Lesson Focus
Many people believe Jesus was God but not human at all. Instead, they believe he just looked and acted like a man.

Lesson Goal
As a result of this session, students will know that Jesus was fully human, that he was God *in the flesh.*

Materials Needed
- For *Optional Media Moments*: CD player and TV, VCR, and video
- For *Optional Opener*: prizes for *A Moving Experience*
- Newspapers and highlighters for *In the Course of Human Events*
- Board (poster board will do) and chalk or marker for *In the Course of Human Events* and *Talk-to*
- Prize for winning team
- Slips of paper with Scripture passages for *Searching for Humanity*
- New Testaments for *Searching for Humanity*
- 3" × 5" index cards and pencils or pens for *Response*

Media Moments ⓂA *(optional)*

Music
- Play "Who But God" by Wes King, from his *A Room Full of Stories* CD, just after the reading of Philippians 2:5-11; or "God Man (Jesus is My Superhero)" by Cadet, on their self-titled CD, *Cadet*.
- Play "Faceless Man" by Creed, from their *Human Clay* CD.
- Play "You Did Not Have a Home" or "Surely God Is With Us" by Rich Mullins and a Ragamuffin Band, from *The Jesus Record* CD during *Response*.

Video
- Play this clip from *The Visual Bible—Matthew*: Matthew 9:18-26 (tape 2– 05:30-08:03–3 minutes). These verses highlight Jesus' compassion—he raises a Jewish leader's daughter and heals a long-sick woman.

Worship Songs
- Choose one of the following songs to sing after the prayer time in *Response:*
  ① "Be Glorified" by Chris Tomlin (on his CD *The Noise We Make*)
  ② "That's Why We Praise Him" by Tommy Walker (on *WOW GREEN WORSHIP* CD taken from *Go the Distance* from Maranatha; originally recorded on *Live at Home* from the C.A. Worship Band with Tommy Walker)

Notes
ⓂA *If you play a CD or a video, be sure to have everything in place and ready to go.*

Real Fun

O P T I O N A L O P E N E R S

A Moving Experience (8 min.)

Make sure that everyone is sitting in rows, facing you, with no gaps between people. Explain that you will be reading a series of descriptions, each with an instruction for changing where they are seated. If a specific description applies to them, students should move according to your instruction. For example, you could say, *"If you received an A on a test last week, move one seat to the right."* Then, whoever fit that description would move one seat to his or her right. Those on the end of a row would go to the opposite end. Explain that if someone is sitting in that spot (in a chair, on the floor, or whatever), they should sit on that person's lap.

Slowly read the descriptions and instructions listed below, allowing time for everyone who is supposed to change seats to make their moves. It may get a little confusing and even wild, with three or four people in one place, but keep moving until it gets so strange or out of control that you have to stop.

If you don't want to be quite so rowdy, read the descriptions without the moving instructions, one at a time, awarding a point value for each one. (Possible point values are included in parentheses.) Then award prizes to those with the most points.

- If you have two or more tooth fillings, *move one seat to the left.* (100)
- If you received a traffic ticket in the last two weeks, *move two seats to the right.* (300)
- If you've received stitches somewhere on your body, *move one seat to the right.* (200)
- If you used an eraser today, *move one seat back.* (100)
- If you've missed a day of school in the last two weeks, *move one seat to the left.* (200)
- If you know a very funny joke, laugh aloud *and move one seat to the left.* (100)
- If you're sleepy, yawn *and move one seat forward.* (100)
- If you have broken something in the last month, *move one seat to the right.* (100)
- If you are a B or better student, *move one seat back.* (200)
- If you've had an operation, *say* "ouch" (don't show us the scar) *and move two seats back.* (300)
- If you've ever been disappointed or depressed over a sports team or game, frown *and move one seat to the left.* (100)

- If you had a haircut last week, pull your hair *and move one seat to the left.* (200)
- If your heart has ever been broken, sigh loudly *and move three seats forward.* (200)
- If you wear glasses, *move one seat to the right.* (100)
- If you're feeling cramped, groan, stretch, *and move one seat to the right.* (100)
- If you can't take this any more, *stand and shout, "I can't take this any more!"*

Opener

In the Course of Human Events (5 to 8 min.)

Divide students into groups of three and give each threesome a newspaper and a highlighter pen. Explain that their assignment is to highlight different human events that are described or pictured in the paper. They should only highlight a specific type of event once.

After a few minutes, have the groups report by having the first group give one event. The subsequent groups can only give events that have not yet been mentioned. As the groups report, write the specific types of events on the board.

"Events" could include crime, pain, death, sex, laughter (also represented by cartoons or comic strips), play, conflict, love, temptation, hunger (also represented by food), birth, marriage, aging, divorce, work, parenting, all the emotions, all the senses, and many others.

Transition (2 to 4 min.)

Explain that, so far, the group has taken a look at what it means to be human. If you used the optional opener, show how all the descriptions were normal human experiences and how many, in fact, could only be experienced by humans. Then say something like this: *These sessions are focusing on Jesus, and last time we discussed the fact that Jesus was and is God. Today, we are looking at the other side of his nature—his humanity. We are going to see that Jesus also was a full-fledged human being; he was man.*

Talking Points (3 to 5 min.)

Ask the following questions and discuss each one briefly:

- **What do you remember from Jesus' life on earth that shows his humanity?** (allow students to answer)
- **How is it possible for Jesus to be both divine and human, God and man?** (allow for response)

Notes

2B *Hopefully, students still will be seated in their threesomes. If not, remember that it takes time to move into and out of groups. Tell them to stay in these groups after this activity.*

2C *Keep these groups in sets of three (not two, four, or whatever). The size of a group determines discussion time.*

2D *Make sure that each threesome has at least one New Testament among them.*

Real Questions

Searching for Humanity — **2B** — **2C** (8 to 11 min.)

Have students return to their threesomes and give each set of three several of the Scripture passages below (with a small group, give each pair more than two passages). Print the passages on separate slips of paper without the answers (the answers are in parentheses after the references). Explain that their assignment is to read the passage, looking for evidence of Jesus' humanity. They should be prepared to share their findings with the whole group.

- John 11:30-37 (Jesus cried) — **2D**
- Luke 4:1-13 (Jesus was tempted)
- John 19:28-30 (Jesus became thirsty)
- Matthew 9:9-13; Luke 24:28-43 (Jesus ate food)
- Matthew 8:23-27 (Jesus slept)
- John 4:1-8 (Jesus became tired; was thirsty)
- John 19:34-37; Hebrews 2:14 (Jesus bled)
- Matthew 4:1-4 (Jesus became hungry)
- Mark 6:1-3; Luke 2:52 (Jesus grew—from a baby to a teenager to an adult)
- Matthew 16:21; John 19:1-3, 16-18; Hebrews 5:8; 1 Peter 4:1 (Jesus suffered)
- Matthew 23:13-22; John 2:13-17 (Jesus became angry)
- Matthew 23:37-39; Mark 6:34; Luke 7:13 (Jesus had compassion)
- John 11:5-7, 36; 13:34; 15:9 (Jesus loved)
- Mark 6:30-34 (Jesus needed rest)
- Mark 15:37-39 (Jesus died)

After a couple of minutes, have the threesomes report their findings, one group at a time. Write their answers on the board.

Talking Points (6 to 8 min.)

Briefly discuss the following questions:

- *In our last meeting, we discussed the implications of Jesus' divinity; that is, the importance for us that Jesus is God. What did we conclude?* **(Answer: He is God in focus, so we can know what God is like; He is the Savior, so we can be saved; He gives us a direct way to God, so we can come directly into his presence.)**
- *Today, we have seen clearly that Jesus is fully human. So what? That is, what difference does that make for us?* **(allow for response)**

Have someone read aloud Philippians 2:5-11:

Your attitude should be the same that Christ Jesus had. Though he was God, he did not demand and cling to his rights as God. He made himself nothing; he took the humble position of a slave and appeared in human form. And in human form he obediently humbled himself even further by dying a criminal's death on a cross. Because of this, God raised him up to the heights of heaven and gave him a name that is above every other name, so that at the name of Jesus every knee will bow, in heaven and on earth and under the earth, and every tongue will confess that Jesus Christ is Lord, to the glory of God the Father. —— **2E**

> **Notes**
>
> **2E** *Print out these passages and give them to selected students before the meeting.*

Thank your reader; then discuss the following questions:

- *What does this passage say about Jesus becoming a human being?* **(Answer:** He willingly gave up the full and unlimited use of his divine attributes, humbling himself completely to become a real human being.**)**
- *What do these verses teach about how we should respond to this truth? That is, what difference should it make in our lives?* **(Answer:** We should have the same attitude of humility and service; that is, we should be like Christ.**)**

Have another student read aloud Hebrews 4:14-16:

That is why we have a great High Priest who has gone to heaven, Jesus the Son of God. Let us cling to him and never stop trusting him. This High Priest of ours understands our weaknesses, for he faced all of the same temptations we do, yet he did not sin. So let us come boldly to the throne of our gracious God. There we will receive his mercy, and we will find grace to help us when we need it.

Again, thank your reader, and, then, briefly discuss this passage using the following questions:

- *What insight does this passage give us about Jesus becoming a human being?* **(Answer:** He understands us completely, even our weaknesses, because he faced all of the temptations that we face.**)** You may also want to look at Hebrews 2:18.
- *What do these verses say should be our response to this truth?* **(Answer:** We should "come boldly" to God, asking for his forgiveness and intervention.**)**

Notes

2F *If you have time, add personal or teenage examples for each main point. That is, you could tell how you experienced pain and sorrow and how Jesus experienced the same thing; you could present typical adolescent temptations and show how Jesus experienced similar ones; and so forth. For WDJD and WWJD, give examples of how that would work.*

Real Jesus

Talk-to   (4 to 6 min.)

Write your main points on the board as you say something like this: *In our last session, we saw that Jesus is divine—he is God. In this meeting, from our close look at Scripture, we have discovered powerful evidence of Jesus' humanity. In other words, Jesus is also fully human. No one knows exactly how that works—it's a God thing. But the evidence leads us to that conclusion: Jesus is the God-man.*

During your study this week, you will learn some personal applications of the fact that Jesus came to earth as a man. Right now, I want to highlight two significant ones.

First, the fact that Jesus was and is a man means that **we know he understands us completely** *(we just read that in Hebrews). Jesus experienced pain, sorrow, joy, frustration, anger, temptation—everything it means to be human, with the exception of sin. Then, on the cross, he went that final step, even experiencing sin and separation from God when he took all of our sins on himself (2 Corinthians 5:21) and became totally, agonizingly separated from his Father (Matthew 27:46). Jesus knows what it means to be a finite human being—he empathizes and sympathizes with us.* **2F**

Because of this, we can talk confidently and honestly with him about anything and everything. And we can bring all of our requests right to the very throne of God.

Second, the truth of the incarnation, that Jesus became a man, means that **he is our example,** *our model. When we want to know what to do in every situation—how to act or react—we can check out how Jesus lived when he was on earth, how he responded to the trials and temptations he faced. When we answer the questions WDJD? (What did Jesus do?) and WWJD? (What would Jesus do?), we will know what we should do.*

Real Life

Response   (6 to 8 min.)

Distribute 3" × 5" index cards and pencils or pens. Instruct students to write, on one side of the card, items of prayer that they will bring honestly and boldly before God this week.

After a couple of minutes, have them turn the cards over. On that side, they should write two moral dilemmas they are facing or probably soon will face. Then, after each one, they should write what they think Jesus would do in that situation.

Have the group reassemble in their groups of three. Ask them to each share one item from both sides of their cards and then pray for each other.

Close (1 min.)

Close by reminding them to interact daily with the devotions in book one of the *Real Life... Real Questions... Real Jesus* series, where they'll meet Lauren the college girl, lonely Carl, Allen the "ex-virgin," and others, who have experienced what it means for Jesus to be human.

Close in prayer.

Junior High Adaptation

A Moving Experience will work well for a while (be sure to eliminate or adapt descriptions that refer to older students), but it will become rowdy in a hurry—so do this quickly. For *In the Course of Human Events,* don't distribute newspapers. Instead, hold up a newspaper, one section at a time, and ask for suggestions of "different human events." In the first discussion, only ask the first question. The threesomes should work all right, but don't insist on only having three in a group (that is, four friends could stay together) and have your adult helpers move through the groups to make sure everyone is on task. In the next discussion, don't discuss the first two questions; instead, give the answers and then move into the discussion of Philippians 2:5-11 and Hebrews 4:14-16.

Knowing the Real Jesus

session 3
Knowing Jesus as Savior

Lesson Texts
Matthew 1:18-25; Mark 8:27-33; various messianic passages in the Old Testament; other passages

Lesson Focus
Many people do not understand Jesus' purpose for coming to the earth as a man. He certainly set a good example to follow and he taught life-changing lessons, but, most importantly, he paid the penalty for sin, dying on the cross in our place.

Lesson Goal
As a result of this session, students will know that Jesus was and is the Savior, the only one who can forgive sin and make people right with God.

Materials Needed
- For *Optional Media Moments*: CD player and TV, VCR, and video
- For *Optional Openers*: prizes and outfits for *Lifeguard Training Course*
- Video recorder, video tape, TV and VCR for *On the Street Interviews*
- Script and reader for *True Identity*
- Bibles for *Talking Points*
- Chalk and chalkboard, or markerboard and markers for *Who Needs a Savior?*
- Sets of Bible passages for *Messiah Search*
- Lifesavers for *Response*

KNOWING THE REAL JESUS 31

Media Moments — 3A (optional)

Music
- Play "Beautiful Savior" by Circadian Rhythm, from their *Over Under Everything* CD, "Less is More" by Relient K, from their release *The Anatomy of the Tongue in Cheek*, or "Song of Love" by Rebecca St. James, on her release *Worship God* during **Response**.

Video
- Play this clip from *The Video Bible–Matthew*: Matthew 26:47–28:1, Jesus' trial, death, and resurrection, Tape 4, 33:28-63:15. (30-minute clip)

Worship Songs
- Choose one of the following songs to sing after the silent prayer in **Response**:
  ① "That's Why We Praise Him," or "Redeemer, Savior, Friend" by Darrell Evans and Chris Springer (on *WOW ORANGE WORSHIP* taken from *B.C.A.D.* from Integrity's Hosanna! Music)
  ② "Shout to the Lord" by Darlene Zschech (on *WOW BLUE WORSHIP* taken from *Shout to the Lord* from Integrity's Hosanna! Music)
  ③ "You Are My King" by Billy James Foote (from *Passion: Better Is One Day* and *Passion: One Day Live* from Sparrow Records)

Notes

3A *If you play a CD or a video, be sure to have everything in place and ready to go.*

Notes

3B *This should work well with any size group and in any size room.*

3C *In case you don't remember Mighty Mouse, you could do something similar (for example, "I'll save you!") in a Dudley Do-Right voice or another cartoon character.*

3D *With a small group, don't do the "elite guards."*

Real Fun

O P T I O N A L   O P E N E R S

Lifeguard Training Course — 3B (6 min.)

Explain that because safety is very important to you in all the group activities, including this one, you want to make sure that they are properly trained as lifeguards. So you are going to take them through a rigorous training regimen. Also, mention that you (and the rest of the staff) will be looking over the group to find a few candidates for the "elite guards"—individuals who perform exceptionally well. Then have everyone stand and take them through the following "training routines."

1. **Muscle Beach**
   Have everyone do bodybuilding poses. Explain that this is very important for lifeguards to gain the respect they need.
2. **Peer Pressure**
   Have everyone shade his or her eyes and peer out over the horizon, as though looking for someone to rescue.
3. **Swim Test**
   Explain that they must demonstrate competency in a number of swimming strokes. Thus, they should perform the strokes (while standing) as you call them out. Call out the following strokes, allowing about five seconds for each one: Australian crawl, butterfly, backstroke, breaststroke, sidestroke, dog paddle, etc.
4. **Reassurance Call**
   Explain that people in need appreciate knowing that help is on the way. So they should sing out (in classic Mighty Mouse fashion), "Here I come to save the day!" — 3C

After leading everyone through the four training routines, choose three to six students to be in the "elite guards," and bring them forward to compete in a contest for the ultimate lifeguard. Then, depending on your time and space available, have them compete in the following activities: *quick change* (see who can don swim trunks, life jacket, sunglasses, and hat the quickest), and *calisthenics workout* (see who can do 10 sit-ups, 10 push-ups, and 10 jumping jacks, doing 10 sets of three, one exercise at a time—one sit-up, one push-up, and one jumping jack in each set). Give the winning student a nice prize; give the other "elite guards" prizes too. — 3D

Woman the Lifeboats (2 min.)

At the beginning of the meeting, after a starter and during a transition when you are talking to the group, have a male student burst into the room and shout frantically (but clearly and distinctly), "Woman the lifeboats! Woman the lifeboats! Woman the lifeboats."

Immediately, you should interrupt him and say, "*Wait a minute—it's not 'Woman the lifeboats,' it's 'Man the lifeboats!'*"

Then, with just a moment's hesitation, the student should reply, "You fill 'em your way, and I'll fill 'em mine!" and then run out of the room.

Openers

On the Street Interviews — 3E (5 to 7 min.)

> **Notes**
> **3E** Make sure that everyone is quiet for **On the Street Interviews** and **True Identity**.

The week before the meeting, take a video recorder to the mall, a busy intersection, or a high school parking lot and ask a number of people this question: "*Who do you think Jesus Christ was?*" You may want to follow up the question with, "*What difference does that make in your life?*"

In the meeting, play the tape, telling students to listen carefully and try to remember the answers to your questions.

True Identity (3 or 4 min.)

Beforehand, photocopy the following script and give it to a student to read through several times. Choose a student who can read with inflection and feeling. Then, immediately following playing the tape for **On the Street Interviews,** have this student come forward and read the script aloud.

This was an unusual collection, walking along together: blue-collar types, professionals, a government worker, and even a political activist—not your normal social grouping. Yet they walked together. Their leader was a teacher or minister of sorts ... and they listened to him, drawn by the power of his personality or the depth of his teachings or some other unknown force ... and they walked together.

Suddenly the teacher stopped, turned, and looked at each one. Quietly he asked: "Who do the people think I am? What are they saying about me?"

"A radical," answered one, "someone like that guy who stirred everyone up outside the city with his wild dress and powerful preaching. Some even say ... a religious nut, fanatic, or cult leader."

"Wait a minute," someone cut in, "not everyone thinks that! I've heard people say that you are a real hero . . . someone they really admire and look up to. They appreciate your moral stance and good example you are setting for their kids. Why, I've even heard comparisons with great men in our history . . . some even think you should lead our country now!"

"My reports haven't been that glowing," said another. "But most of the people I know think you are a great teacher. You help them see life differently, and you stretch their minds. They really enjoy listening to you and say that they learn a lot."

Others peppered him with other answers—public impressions and ideas of this man they respected and loved.

Then the teacher got everyone's full attention again and asked: "Who do you think I am?"

And it was silent.

"What kind of question is that?" they thought. "Does he think we don't know or that we question his authority?" And in the silence, they groped for the correct answer to give.

· · · · · · · · · ·

"Who do you think I am? Who do you say I am?" he asks us. And we sort through our ideas and theological categories to give him a "right" answer.

Who do you think he is? Do you know? What difference does it make?

Real Questions

Talking Points   (3 to 5 min.)

Thank your reader; then ask if anyone recognized the story modernized by the reader. The passage was Matthew 16:13-15.

Make sure that everyone has access to a Bible and have them turn to Mark 8:27-33. Show how the answers given by the disciples to Jesus' question parallel those in the reading. (John the Baptist = "radical," "religious nut," "cult leader"; Elijah = "real hero," "great man in history"; one of the other prophets = "great teacher," etc.)

KNOWING THE REAL JESUS | 35

Then say something like this: *As we heard from the taped interviews and from the reading, people have many ideas about Jesus' true identity. Many of those views are correct, in part. That is, Jesus certainly was a radical, a hero, and a great teacher. But all of those descriptions miss the main reason that Jesus came to earth. According to the passage in Mark, what was that?* (Answer: "Peter replied, 'You are the Messiah'" [verse 29].)

Ask: *Who was the "Messiah"? What did the Jewish people expect this person to be like?* Discuss briefly. **Answers may include, "a military hero who would free them from Roman rule," "someone like King David or King Solomon who would restore Israel to its former glory and power,"** and so forth.

> **Notes**
>
> **3F** *If you have this meeting near Christmas or Easter, you will have many examples from songs and other worship elements.*

Who Needs a Savior? (5 to 7 min.)

Say: *Now I'd like us to look at this from a different angle.*

Then ask: *In addition to the religion section or stories about religion, in what newspaper articles might you find the word "savior"?*

Note their answers, either writing them on a sheet of paper or listing them on the board for your reference later. Their answers could include the following:

- Sports—an athlete could be called a team's "savior" for scoring a winning basket, touchdown, run, point, or goal or for making a crucial defensive stop.
- Business—a new CEO could be described as the hoped-for "savior" of a company.
- World events—a war hero who liberated a city or nation from tyranny could be called a "savior."
- Politics—a high-ranking government official, newly elected by a landslide, could be described as his or her party's "savior."

Next, ask: *What do these "saviors" have in common?* **(Answer: they seem to refer to rescuing and turning defeat into victory.)**

Then ask: *Almost all of the news stories about saviors refer to groups being "saved" by the heroic actions of an individual. What other illustrations can you think of that would be more personal; that is, an individual person might be personally and individually "saved" by someone?* **(Possible answers could include a drowning person saved by a lifeguard, a choking restaurant patron saved by someone doing the Heimlich maneuver, a child saved from a speeding car by a quick-thinking crossing guard, a dying person saved by a doctor using a new medicine or medical procedure, and so forth.)**

Notes

3G Remember, it takes time to move into and out of groups, so divide quickly.

Messiah Search — 3G   (6 to 9 min.)

Divide students into two groups. Assign an adult leader to each group and give each one a set of Bible passages (see below) to read and discuss. Each group should decide how the Messiah is pictured in their passages and be ready to report their findings to everyone.

GROUP 1
Numbers 24:15-19
Deuteronomy 18:15-19
Isaiah 9:6-7
Jeremiah 23:5-8
Daniel 7:13-14
Micah 5:2-5
Zechariah 9:9

GROUP 2
Psalm 22:1-8
Psalm 41:9
Psalm 69:19-21
Psalm 118:22-24
Isaiah 50:6
Isaiah 53:1-12
Zechariah 12:10-11

Messiah Findings   (5 to 7 min.)

Have Group 1 report. Afterward, explain that this was the Messiah for whom the Jewish people were looking, a conquering king. A hero, military leader, much like the kinds of people reported in the news as "saviors." When Jesus failed to meet these expectations, the people rejected him.

Next, have Group 2 report their findings. Afterward, point out the contrast. These passages pictured the Messiah as suffering and dying (the "Suffering Servant"). Show how these Old Testament passages almost sound like play-by-play descriptions of Jesus' life and death.

Then say something like this: *We found two types of prophetic descriptions of the Messiah in the Old Testament. The first group read passages that describe the Messiah as the King, a powerful ruler over individuals and nations. But the second group read passages that describe him as the Suffering Servant, dying on behalf of individuals and the nation. Both are*

KNOWING THE REAL JESUS

true. When Jesus came the first time, he came to suffer and die. But one day he will return to judge and rule.

In this meeting, our activities and discussions have centered around two words: Messiah and Savior. We have taken a close look at "Messiah," but what about Savior? How does that concept relate? In other words, what do we mean when we say Jesus is our Savior? *Allow several students to respond.*

Real Jesus

Talk-to (4 or 5 min.)

Say something like this: *Matthew 1:18-25 tells us the story of Jesus' birth. Listen carefully*:

"Now this is how Jesus the Messiah was born. His mother, Mary, was engaged to be married to Joseph. But while she was still a virgin, she became pregnant by the Holy Spirit. Joseph, her fiancé, being a just man, decided to break the engagement quietly, so as not to disgrace her publicly.

As he considered this, he fell asleep, and an angel of the Lord appeared to him in a dream. 'Joseph, son of David,' the angel said, 'do not be afraid to go ahead with your marriage to Mary. For the child within her has been conceived by the Holy Spirit. And she will have a son, and you are to name him Jesus, for he will save his people from their sins.' All of this happened to fulfill the Lord's message through his prophet:

"Look! The virgin will conceive a child! She will give birth to a son, and he will be called Immanuel (meaning, God is with us). When Joseph woke up, he did what the angel of the Lord commanded. He brought Mary home to be his wife, but she remained a virgin until her son was born. And Joseph named him Jesus."

If you were listening carefully, you heard the two concepts that we have been discussing: Messiah and Savior. Matthew wrote: "Now this is how Jesus the Messiah was born." Then, the angel who announced the birth to Joseph said, "for he will save his people from their sins." So from even before Jesus was born, the word was out that he was the promised Messiah and the Savior of the world.

The point could not be clearer—Jesus' purpose for coming to earth was to **save people from their sins**. Why do people need to be saved? Why do they need a Savior? Because, without a Savior they are separated from God, dying

Notes

3H *If you are pretty sure that non-Christians are in the group, spend more time on this part of your talk.*

in their sins, doomed. Romans 6:23 states this very clearly: "For the wages of sin is death, but the free gift of God is eternal life through Christ Jesus our Lord." His death paid the penalty for our sins.

Some people don't think they need a Savior. They think, "I'm not so bad. After all, I've never robbed a bank, bombed a building, or killed anyone." By comparing themselves to someone really bad, they feel better about themselves and excuse their actions. But what happens when we compare ourselves to God who is perfect and holy? Whoa, do we fall short! Even one tiny sin drops us way out of contention for heaven. And think about it—every one of us is way worse than that. You're all good kids, and I'm a pretty nice person myself, but we all are totally corrupt, filthy, and sinful when compared to God's perfect standard.

That's why Christ came. Jesus, fully God, entered our world, fully human. He lived, ate, interacted with people, and experienced every possible temptation, yet he did not sin. He lived the only perfect life ever lived on earth.

Then, even though he did not deserve it, Jesus paid the ultimate price for sin—death—physical and spiritual death. Listen to his anguish on the cross as he became totally separated from his Father: "My God, my God, why have you forsaken me?" (Matthew 27:46)

He was taking our place, your place, as the Savior . . . your Savior.

So what does this mean for you right here, right now? During the week, your daily readings will highlight several implications for our lives; right now let's look at two.

First, it means that if you have never trusted in Christ as your personal Savior, you need to do so as soon as possible. ——**3H**

Second, if you do know Christ as Savior, you should be thinking of those with whom you can share this great news. In other words, who needs to hear that Christ can be their Savior too?

Real Life

Response (4 to 6 min.)

Help everyone find a quiet place, apart from anyone else. Tell them to spend some time with God, talking to him about the points you just covered. That is, if they don't know Christ as Savior, they should talk with God about that.

They could share their doubts or questions with him, or they could give their lives to him.

Or they can pray about having the courage and opportunity to share the Good News with others—friends and family members who don't yet know the Savior.

After a couple of minutes of silent prayer, get everyone's attention. Tell them that you and other adult leaders are ready and willing to talk with them further about these issues. All they have to do is ask.

Encourage everyone to read the devotions for the week where they will read about other students who learned what it means that Christ is Savior.

As everyone leaves, give each person a roll of Lifesavers to remind them of the lesson.

Close (1 min.)

Remind students of the lives they will meet this week during their devotional time from book one in the *Real Life . . . Real Questions . . . Real Jesus* series, and how these young adults met Jesus as Savior. They'll encounter Kim's tough question, Serena's desire for forgiveness, and more.

Close in prayer.

Junior High Adaptation

This meeting may prove to be too conceptual for many junior high students. To minimize this problem, don't spend much time on the Jewish concept of Messiah. Instead, focus on Savior, using the **Lifeguard Training Course** but not the "elite guards" and **Woman the Lifeboats**. Next, move directly to the **Who Needs a Savior?** discussion. Then, instead of dividing into two groups, only use the Scripture passages for **Group 2** and discuss them as a whole group. The rest of the meeting should work well as written.

Knowing the Real Jesus

session 4
Knowing Jesus as King

Lesson Texts
Selected passages

Lesson Focus
Many people profess Christ as their "personal Savior," but then seem to forget that he is also "Lord." They want to be saved from sin and its consequences but are reluctant to revere Jesus as their King and obey his commands.

Lesson Goal
As a result of this session, students will know that Jesus was and is the King, the ruler of the universe and the Lord of their lives who will return to earth one day as righteous judge.

Materials Needed
- For *Optional Media Moments*: CD player and TV, VCR, and video
- For *Optional Openers*: pencils/pens, quizzes, and prizes for *King Me!* Prepared sets of instructions, envelopes, and prizes for *Orders from Headquarters*
- Noise-making devices for *Royal Jeopardy*
- Prizes for *Royal Jeopardy*
- Burger King crown for *Royal Jeopardy*
- Blackboard and chalk or markerboard for *Royal Jeopardy*
- Pens/pencils for *Jesus Rules!*
- *Jesus Rules!* worksheets for *Jesus Rules!*
- Bibles for *Jesus Rules!*

Media Moments — 4A (optional)

Music
- Play "I'm Not the King" by Audio Adrenaline, from their *Bloom* CD. It's a great upbeat song that will wake your students up.
- Another song that deals with **Christ's authority** is "Jesus Christ" by Among Thorns, on their *Desperate* CD.

Video
- Show a video with short clips of kings and emperors from a variety of films such as *Princess Bride*, *The Last Emperor*, *Anna and the King*, *Gladiator*, *Shrek*, and so forth, after **Royal Jeopardy** and just before **Talking Points**.

Worship Songs
- Choose one of the following songs and sing after **Response** and before **Close:**
  ① "Shout to the Lord," "That's Why We Praise Him," "You Are My King" (Foote), "Victory Chant" by Joseph Vogels (on *WOW ORANGE WORSHIP* taken from *The Lord Reigns* from Integrity)
  ② "You Are My King" by Brian Doerksen (from *Surrender* from Vineyard UK)
  ③ "Great Are You" by downhere, on their self-titled debut release or "Wonderful King" by the David Crowder Band, on their release *Can You Hear Us?*

Notes

4A *If you play a CD or a video, be sure to have everything in place and ready to go.*

Notes

> **4B** Don't take too long on this (it's an **Opener**), especially when giving the correct answers. Some will argue that their answers are correct or that your questions are too hard—keep it moving.

Real Fun

O P T I O N A L   o p e n e r s

King Me! ──── 4B (7 min.)

Ahead of time, you will need to make enough photocopies of the following quiz for all your students to have one. Distribute pencils or pens and this matching quiz. Award prizes to those who get the most correct answers (in parentheses). Obviously, their copies won't have the answer in parentheses!

KING ME!

Match the clues on the left with the people, events, etc. on the right (one for each).

1. civil rights champion (H.)
2. "King of the world" (K.)
3. "unforgettable" (B.)
4. "King of Soul" (I.)
5. "The King" (O.)
6. skyscraper climber (L.)
7. "of Orient are" (M.)
8. hamburger haven (E.)
9. tennis star (J.)
10. love those pucks (Q.)
11. "King of the Road" (P.)
12. "Lion King" (C.)
13. had some bad knights (F.)
14. scary writer (A.)
15. took place in Siam (N.)
16. stumped the "Kings horses and men" (G.)
17. NBA associate (D.)

A. Stephen King
B. Nat King Cole
C. Simba
D. The Sacramento Kings
E. Burger King
F. King Arthur
G. Humpty Dumpty
H. Martin Luther King, Jr.
I. Otis Redding
J. Billy Jean King
K. "Titanic"
L. King Kong
M. "We Three Kings"
N. *The King & I*
O. Elvis Presley
P. Roger Miller
Q. The Los Angeles Kings

Orders from Headquarters (5 min.)

Before the session, prepare multiple sets of instructions and envelopes. Put a set of instructions in each envelope, and on the outside of the envelopes, write "Sealed Orders" or "Orders from Headquarters." Make sure you have enough envelopes so that everyone in the group will receive one. With a larger group, you can have students work in pairs, with each pair receiving an envelope (in this case, both people in the pair must follow all the instructions in their envelope). Each set should have three instructions, and all of the sets should be different. Here are some possible sets of instructions to use:

SET ONE
- Shake the right hand of ten different people in the room.
- Do 15 jumping jacks.
- Find someone whose birthday is today or very close to today (other than you) and have them sign here: _____.

SET TWO
- Write a short poem about a king in this space.
- Sing "Happy Birthday to Me" at the top of your lungs.
- Line up five students by height (not including you) and have them put their initials here: ____ ____ ____ ____ ____.

SET THREE
- Find three people with unusual middle names (other than you) and write those middle names here: _____.
- Spin counterclockwise ten times.
- Tell four students and two adults how much you love your country.

SET FOUR
- Pretend to weep, loudly and uncontrollably, for ten seconds.
- Have someone of the opposite sex give you a 15-second shoulder massage.
- Write the names of five Old Testament kings here: _____
_____.

SET FIVE
- Teach two other students a secret handshake with at least four movements in it.
- Lie on the floor and do 20 ab scrunches.
- Run to another room and yell, "Hey everybody—come in here!"

SET SIX
- Find someone (other than you) who has met a top leader in our national government and have that person sign here: _____.
- Find someone who will count for you as you do ten push-ups.
- One at a time, go to five members of the opposite sex, kiss their hand, look them in the eye, and say very sincerely and warmly, "Thank you for coming."

Set Seven
- Walk at a leisurely pace around the perimeter of the room, smiling and waving as though you are the homecoming queen or king and in a parade.
- Jump up and down ten times while yelling, "I'm tall! Really tall!"
- Get four people to tell you what a great person you are.

Set Eight
- Go to five students, one at a time, look them in the eye and say with conviction while shaking your finger at them, "If I've told you once, I've told you a million times—don't exaggerate!"
- Get six others to let you leapfrog over them.
- Ask two adults for their mothers' maiden names. Write those names here: _____.

Set Nine
- Lie down in the middle of the room and pretend to sleep for 15 seconds.
- Find a partner and waltz around the perimeter of the room one time.
- Yell loudly, "It's around me! It's all around me!" until someone asks, "What? What's around you" (or something similar). Then answer, "my belt!"

Add as many sets of instructions as you need. Feel free to repeat instructions, but make sure that no two sets are alike. Distribute the envelopes to the individuals or pairs. Explain that when you give the signal, they should tear open their envelopes and follow their orders. When they have finished, they should run to the front of the room and then sit quietly. You will note the order of finish. The first persons to correctly follow their orders will receive prizes.

Give the signal and begin. Note: be sure to have plenty of prizes because several individuals or pairs will claim to finish first.

The General Idea   (5 min.)

Recruit an adult in your church or neighborhood who is serving or who has served in the military—ideally someone who is or was an officer. Introduce the person to the group, giving his or her credentials. Then interview your special guest, using the following questions:

- *How long have you served in the military?*
- *What made you choose that career?*
- *Why is the chain of command so important in the military?*
- *How are (or were) you supposed to respond to a superior officer?*

- *How are (or were) you expected to react to orders?*
- *What do (or did) you like best about being given orders from others?*
- *What do (or did) you like least about that?*
- *Why is discipline so important in the military?*

Opener

Royal Jeopardy *(8 to 10 min.)*

Choose three or four students to compete in a game of "Jeopardy." Give each one a noise-making device (whistle, bell, horn, buzzer, clicker, etc.). Explain that you will read aloud a clue relating to an historical royal figure. If they know the person to whom the clue relates, they should make their sound (blow the whistle, ring the bell, and so forth). Then, when you call on them (the first person to respond), they should give their answer in the form of a question. For example, "Who was King Ferdinand?" or "Who was Prince Paul?" or "Who was Queen Latifa?" Award 2000 points for every correct answer and subtract 1000 points for every incorrect answer. When a contestant answers incorrectly, give the second person who responded the chance to answer, awarding 1000 points for a correct answer and no penalty for an incorrect one. Ask a student to keep score on a blackboard or white markerboard. Afterward, announce the winner as "King or Queen of the Group," place a Burger King crown on his or her head, and give him or her a prize, such as a "King Don." Here are some clues to use (the correct answers are in parentheses). ─── **4C**

- The first king of Israel **(Who was Saul?)**
- His Egyptian artifacts made a U.S. tour **(Who was King Tut?)**
- Popular ruler of Jordan **(Who was King Hussein?)**
- Gave Daniel fits **(Who was King Nebuchadnezzar?)**
- Elizabeth II **(Who is Queen of England?)**
- Mordecai's courageous cousin **(Who was Queen Esther?)**
- Colonists rebelled against him **(Who was King George III?)**
- The wisest man who ever lived **(Who was King Solomon?)**
- A contemporary English icon who died tragically **(Who was Princess Di?)**
- Shakespeare's gloomy prince **(Who was Hamlet?)**
- A man after God's own heart **(Who was King David?)**
- Strategized the path to power **(Who was Prince Machiavelli?)**
- Phil and Betsy's son **(Who is Prince Charles?)** Note: Phil = Philip and Betsy = Elizabeth
- Pilate's associate **(Who was King Herod?)**

Notes

4C *Again, this could take longer than necessary if students contest your judgments. Make it fun by awarding bonus points for nice smile, good attitude, great style in using the noise-maker, and so forth, and keep it moving.*

- Former movie star who married in Monaco **(Who was Princess Grace?)**
- Had a wicked wife, Jezebel **(Who was King Ahab?)**
- Awoke Snow White **(Who was Prince Charming?)**
- Young heir to the British throne **(Who is Prince William?)**

Transition   *(1 min.)*

Congratulate the winner. Then say something like this: *The focus of our sessions has been discovering the "real Jesus." That is, we have been looking beyond the hype and misconceptions to who Jesus really is. We have discovered that he is fully God and fully man, both divine and human. And we've seen that the main purpose for his coming to earth was to die on the cross in our place, to save us from our sins—he is our Savior. Today, we're going to look at Jesus again and see another, powerful aspect of his person. You can probably guess from our opening activity—Jesus as King.*

Talking Points   *(3 to 5 min.)*

Continue: *Last time, we discussed the Jewish concept of Messiah. Just to review, what kind of Messiah were the Jews expecting?* Discuss this briefly. **(Answer: a deliverer; a mighty conqueror; a king, like David or Solomon.)**

Say: *A Jew in the time of Christ, then, would picture his "king" as the Messiah—a powerful, just, and righteous ruler. What about a Greek or Roman person back then—what do you think his concept of "king" might include?* Discuss briefly. **(Possible answers: certainly a powerful man, probably a tyrant, like the Roman emperors; a warrior/soldier who defeated enemies and subjugated them.)**

Then ask: *OK, that was back then, but what about today? What do you think most people in our society think of when they hear the title "king"?* Again, discuss this briefly. **(Possible answers: a figurehead of government, like the royal family in England, with little power or authority.)** *How about the word "Lord"—what do most people think that word means?* **(Answer: it's not used much, except when talking about "lords and ladies" of the past or "landlord.")**

Commend everyone on their answers and explain that they will be taking a close look at Scripture to see what Jesus meant when he said he was "King" and "Lord."

KNOWING THE REAL JESUS | 49

Real Questions

Jesus Rules! — 4D (8 to 12 min.)

Divide into three groups, and, if possible, assign an adult leader to each group to lead the discussion. Distribute *Jesus Rules!* worksheets (a master to photocopy is at the end of the lesson) and pens/pencils to everyone. Also, make sure that everyone has access to a Bible.

Assign each group to one of the three sections of the worksheet. Students should look up the passages and discuss them one at a time, first looking for the people involved in the story, then the place, and, finally, the plot or main conflict. The leader or a student should be prepared to share the answers of the smaller group with the large group.

Here's a worksheet with possible answers in italics. — 4E

> **4D** *Remember, it takes time to move into and out of groups.*
>
> **4E** *Brief your group leaders ahead of time, so they are prepared for the worksheet and discussion.*

Jesus Rules!

	PEOPLE	PLACE	PLOT
THE KING Matthew 2:1-18	*Jesus, wise men, Herod, priests, teachers, Mary, Joseph, soldiers, boys*	*Jerusalem palace, Bethlehem house and city*	*Herod was threatened by the possibility of a new king*
Matthew 26:62-64	*Jesus, high priest, false witnesses, council*	*high priest's house— on trial*	*Jesus is asked if he is Messiah; he answers yes*
Matthew 27:11, 27-31, 37	*Jesus, Pilate, soldiers, two criminals, crowd*	*Pilate's house, soldiers' headquarters, cross*	*Pilate asks if Jesus is king of the Jews; Jesus says yes; Soldiers mock*

Notes

	PEOPLE	PLACE	PLOT
Romans 10:9-12	Paul, Roman believers	Paul wrote this letter in Greece before leaving for Jerusalem	Paul highlights the necessity of professing Jesus as Lord
Revelation 15:3; 19:11-16	John, seven angels, the victorious saints, Jesus	vision of heaven, crystal sea	Jesus is revealed as "King of kings and Lord of lords"

The KINGDOM

	PEOPLE	PLACE	PLOT
Luke 1:29-33	Gabriel, Mary	Nazareth, Mary's house	Gabriel tells Mary her son Jesus will reign over Israel "forever"
Matthew 10:7; 13:11	Jesus, 12 disciples	outside Capernaum; at the shore	Jesus tells the disciples to announce that the Kingdom is near
Luke 17:20-21	Jesus, Pharisees, disciples	on the way to Jerusalem	Jesus says the Kingdom has no visible signs and is among them
John 18:33-37	Pilate, Jesus	in Pilate's house	Jesus says his Kingdom is not of this world
Revelation 1:6	John, the 7 churches in Asia	island of Patmos	John says believers are Christ's kingdom

The SUBJECTS

	PEOPLE	PLACE	PLOT
Matthew 7:21-27; Luke 6:46	Jesus, disciples, crowds	Mt. of Olives, near Kidron Valley	The decisive issue for kingdom membership is obedience to the Father

KNOWING THE REAL JESUS 51

	PEOPLE	PLACE	PLOT	Notes
John 3:1-21	Jesus, Nicodemus	Jerusalem, at night, in a house	Jesus says the only way into the Kingdom is to be born again	**4F** Collect the pens and pencils.
John 14:15, 21	Jesus, 11 disciples	Jerusalem, after the last supper	Jesus says that those who truly love him obey his commandments	
Philippians 2:5-11	Paul, believers at Philippi	Paul is writing from prison in Rome	Paul says everyone will bow to Jesus and confess him as Lord	
Colossians 2:6-7	Paul, believers at Colosse	Paul is writing from prison in Rome	Paul tells believers to continue to obey Jesus their Lord	

Talking Points —— **4F** (6 to 10 min.)

Bring everyone back together and have the groups report their answers, one group at a time. Encourage everyone to fill in the answers for the sections that weren't assigned.

Commend everyone for their good work, and explain that you want them to summarize their findings. Then ask:

- *What did we discover about Jesus as "King"?* **(Answer: He is King of kings and Lord of lords.)**
- *What did we learn about the nature of Christ's kingdom?* **(Answer: His Kingdom is in the hearts of all who trust in him as Savior.)**
- *What did we find out about the subjects of the Kingdom?* **(Answer: Kingdom subjects, Christ's true followers, obey him.)**

Then say: *C. S. Lewis has written a set of delightful children's stories entitled* The Chronicles of Narnia—*you may have read them. In the first book,* The Lion, the Witch, and the Wardrobe, *Peter, Lucy, Edmund, and Susan (four children) are exploring the Narnia countryside when they come upon some Beavers. Mr. and Mrs. Beaver invite them home for dinner. After the meal,* they are discussing the situation in Narnia when Aslan is mentioned. Aslan is the most important character in the Chronicles, a powerful lion and a picture of Christ.

Mr. Beaver explains that when Aslan returns, everything will be made right. Then Lucy asks: "Is—is he a man?"

"Aslan a man!" said Mr. Beaver sternly. "Certainly not. I tell you he is the King of the wood and the son of the great Emperor-Beyond-the-Sea. Don't you know who is the King of the Beasts? Aslan is a lion—the Lion, the great Lion."

"Ooh!" said Susan, "I'd thought he was a man. Is he . . . quite safe? I shall feel rather nervous about meeting a lion."

"That you will, dearie, and no mistake," said Mrs. Beaver, "if there's anyone who can appear before Aslan without their knees knocking, they're either braver than most or else just silly."

"Then he isn't safe?" said Lucy.

"Safe?" said Mr. Beaver. "Don't you hear what Mrs. Beaver tells you? Who said anything about safe? Course he isn't safe. But he's good. He's the King, I tell you."

Then ask:

- *What did Mr. Beaver mean when he said, "Course he isn't safe. But he's good"?* (Answer: Aslan isn't safe in that he is tame and controlled, so the children must take him seriously and never take him for granted. But he is good and can be trusted to act in their best interests.)
- *How might it help us if we applied that statement to Jesus?* (Answer: Jesus is the King, and we are his subjects. Jesus is in control, not us, and we should never take him lightly. Instead, we must trust and obey him totally and without reservation.)

Real Jesus

Talk-to (4 or 5 min.)

Say something like this: *In our last four sessions, we have taken a very close look at Jesus' true identity. Many people have a totally wrong or a partial idea of who Jesus is, but we've looked at Scripture to discover the truth.*

We have seen that Jesus is God, and that he is man—the God-man. He loves us, knows us completely, and experienced everything that it means to be human. He identifies and empathizes with us—he is one of us.

We have also seen that Jesus is the Savior of all who put their trust in him. His main purpose in coming to earth was to take our sins on himself—to become sin—and then to pay the penalty for sin. When Jesus died on the cross, he died for us, in our place. Knowing Jesus as Savior means that we are free from the power and penalty of sin and that we have eternal life.

Today, we have seen that Jesus is King. In Colossians 1:15-20, Paul pulls it all together when he writes: "Christ is the visible image of the invisible God. He existed before God made anything at all and is supreme over all creation. Christ is the one through whom God created everything in heaven and earth. He made the things we can see and the things we can't see—kings, kingdoms, rulers, and authorities. Everything has been created through him and for him. He existed before everything else began, and he holds all creation together.

"Christ is the head of the church, which is his body. He is the first of all who will rise from the dead, so he is first in everything. For God in all his fullness was pleased to live in Christ, and by him God reconciled everything to himself. He made peace with everything in heaven and on earth by means of his blood on the cross."

Did you hear that? Christ "made peace with everything in heaven and on earth by means of his blood on the cross" and he "is supreme over all creation." He is our Savior and our King.

To acknowledge and honor Christ as King demands that we not take him for granted in our lives and treat him as an accessory or add-on. Instead, we must honor him as Lord and do what he tells us to do.

Real Life

Response   (4 to 6 min.)

Have everyone find a place in the room where they can be alone, not touching someone else, and away from distractions. Tell them to spend a few minutes talking to God about their relationship with him. They may have to do the following:

- Confess the fact that they aren't honoring Christ as their King and where they have knowingly disobeyed him.
- Ask God to show them what he wants them to do.

After a few minutes of silent prayer, lead everyone in singing together, "I Love You, Lord," "Majesty," or a similar song of dedication to Christ as Lord.

Close   (1 min.)

Close by explaining that this week's devotions from book one in the *Real Life . . . Real Questions . . . Real Jesus* series will help them do what they prayed. During this week they will read how Jamal, Lanie, Toby, and others worked it out.

Close with prayer.

Junior High Adaptation

For your opener, use *King Me!* and substitute a few easier questions for some of the more difficult ones. Then move directly to the discussion, beginning with a question or two about kings and lords. For *Jesus Rules!* go ahead and divide into three groups, but have the adult leader lead the discussion and fill in the answers on a worksheet instead of distributing paper to everyone. For *Response*, enforce them finding a place to *be alone, not touching someone else*. At this point, you may have to separate friends.

Jesus Rules!

Read the following passages and write down who are the people involved in each passage, where the action takes place, and what is the plot, or main conflict, in each. Look for how Jesus is portrayed as king, how his kingdom is depicted, and how his subjects are described.

	PEOPLE	PLACE	PLOT
THE KING Matthew 2:1-18 Matthew 26:62-64 Matthew 27:11, 27-31, 37 Romans 10:9-12 Revelation 15:3; 19:11-16			
THE KINGDOM Luke 1:29-33 Matthew 10:7; 13:11 Luke 17:20-21 John 18:33-37 Revelation 1:6			
THE SUBJECTS Matthew 7:21-27; Luke 6:46 John 3:1-21 John 14:15, 21 Philippians 2:5-11 Colossians 2:6-7			

© 2002 by Standard Publishing. Permission is granted to reproduce this page for ministry purposes only—not for resale.

meet the Real Jesus

See His Passion

Sense His Presence

Feel His Love

Open the pages of the *Jesus Bible* and come face to face with the Savior. Learn unXpected facts about Jesus. Connect with others just like you by reading their Real Xpressions. Xalt Him through all the names, titles, and descriptions of Jesus. And Xplicit Answers will point you to solutions to life's toughest problems.

NEW LIVING TRANSLATION
for those who thirst.

The *Jesus Bible*.
Available wherever Bibles are sold.

TYNDALE

www.newlivingtranslation.com